Together

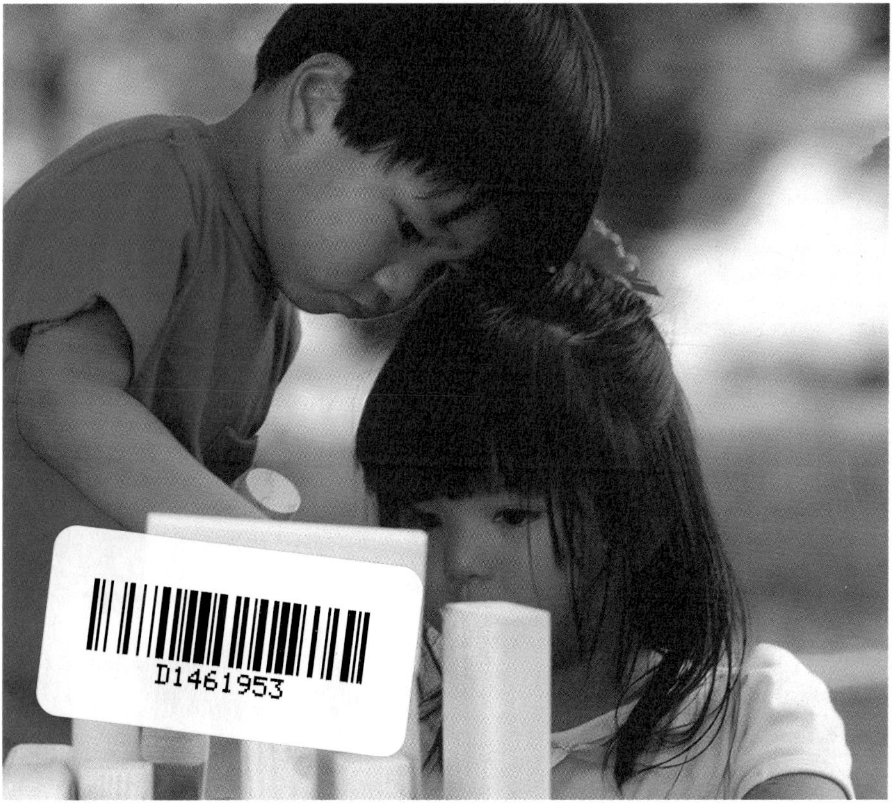

Judy Nayer

We can plant a garden.

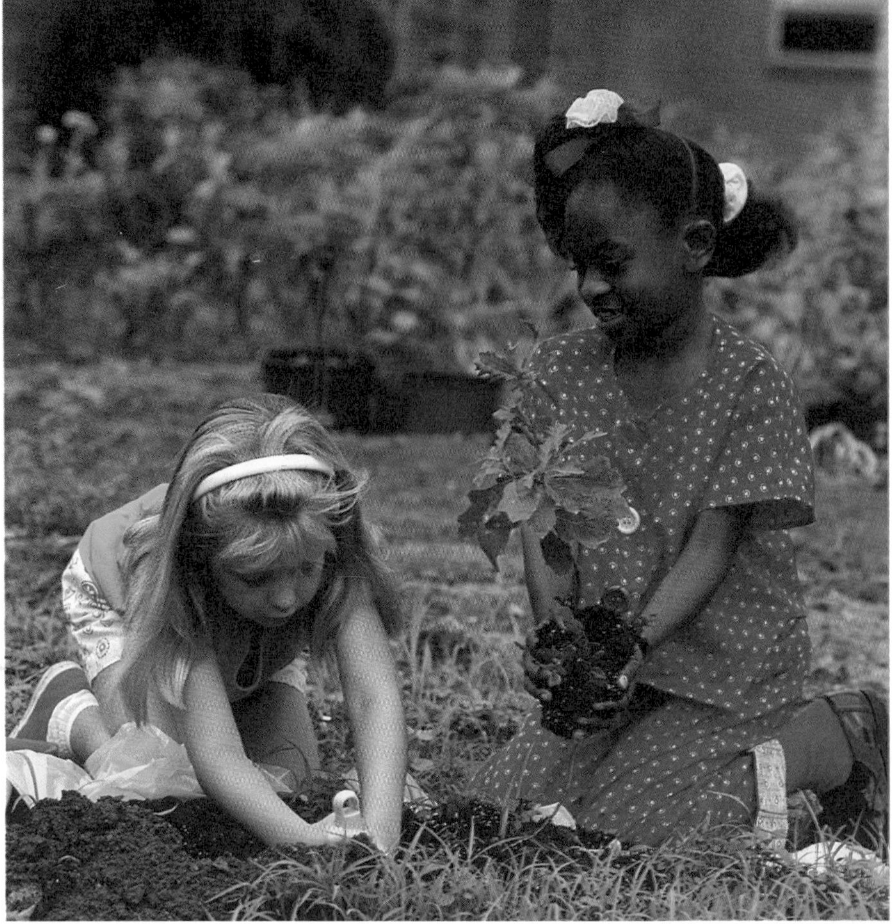

We can paint a mural.

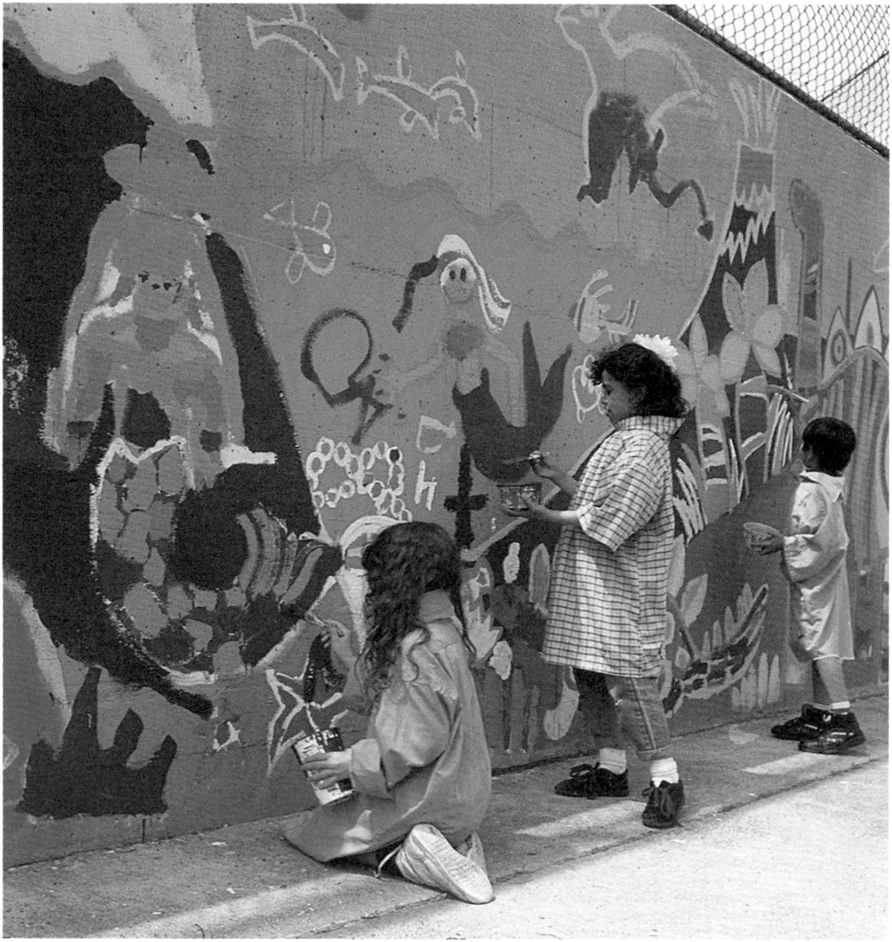

We can sing in a chorus.

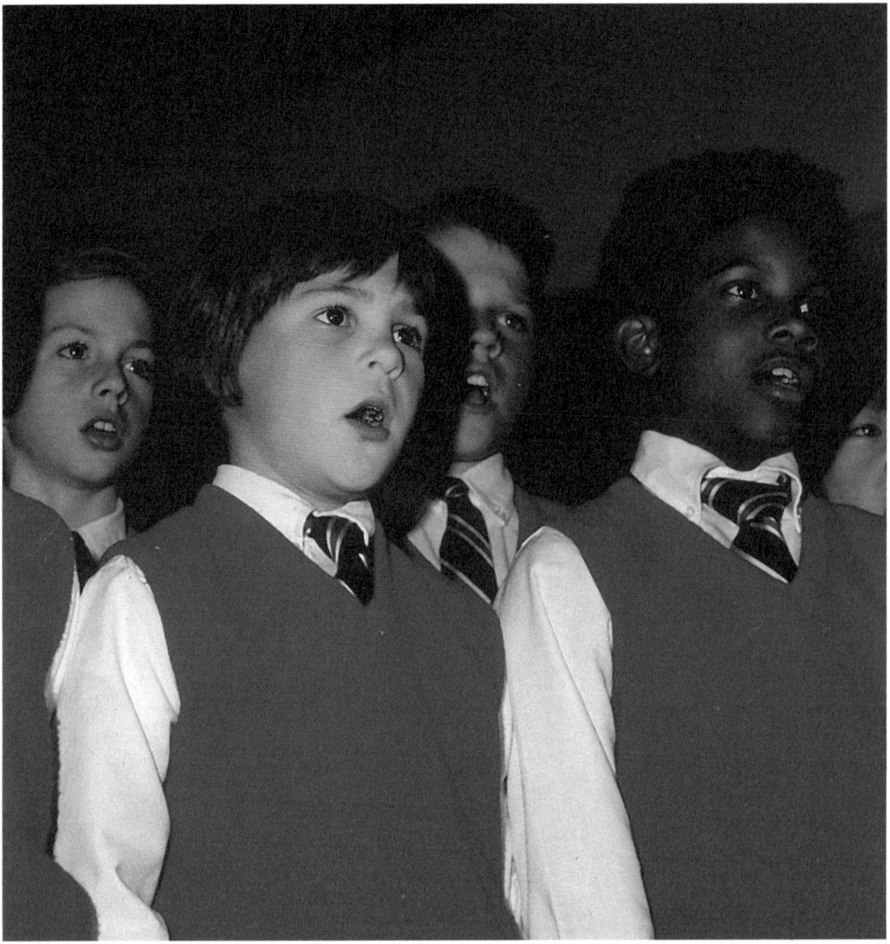

We can play on a team.

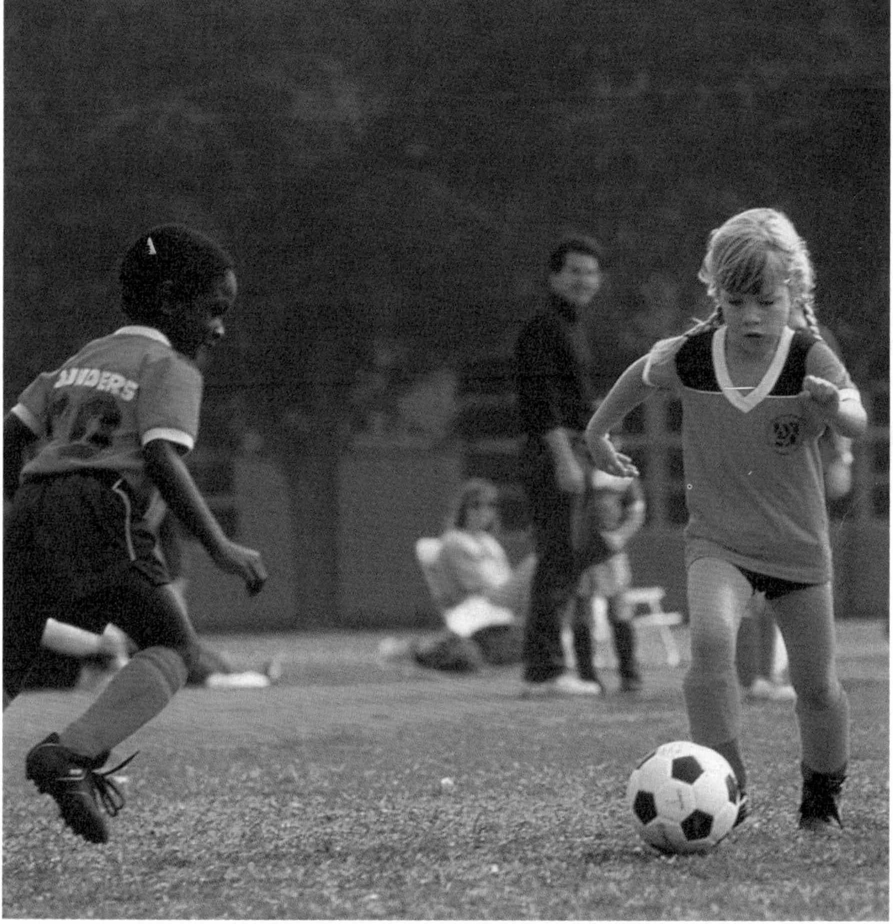

We can clean up the beach.

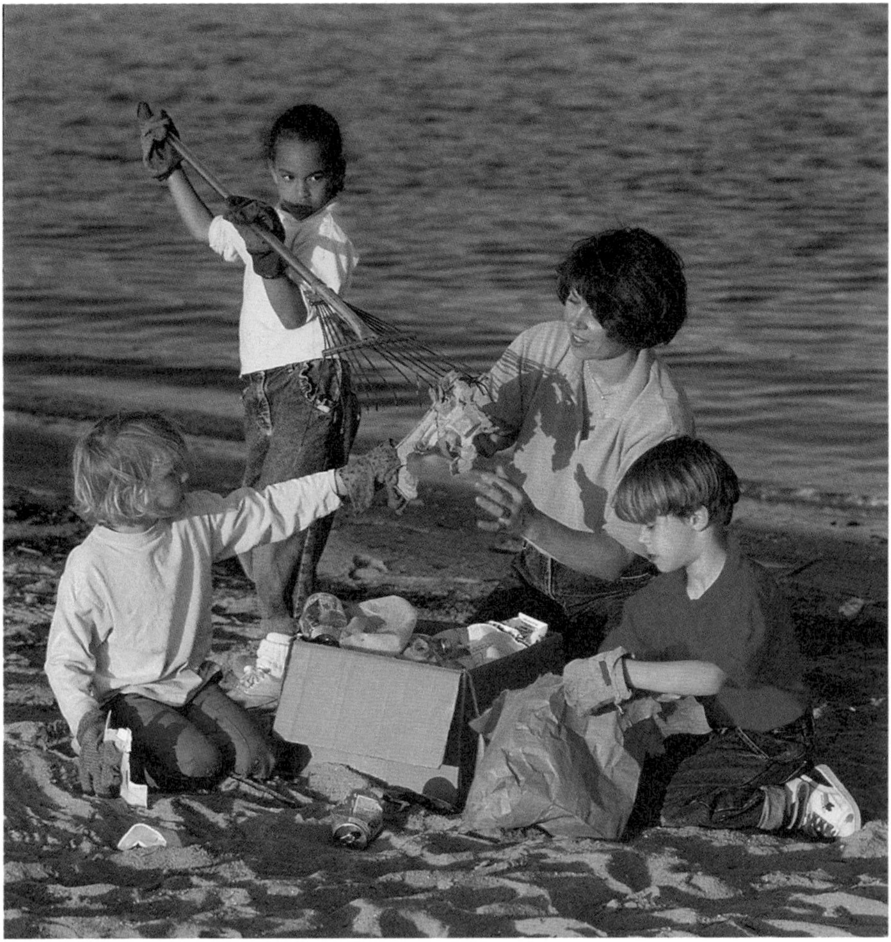

We can fix this bike.

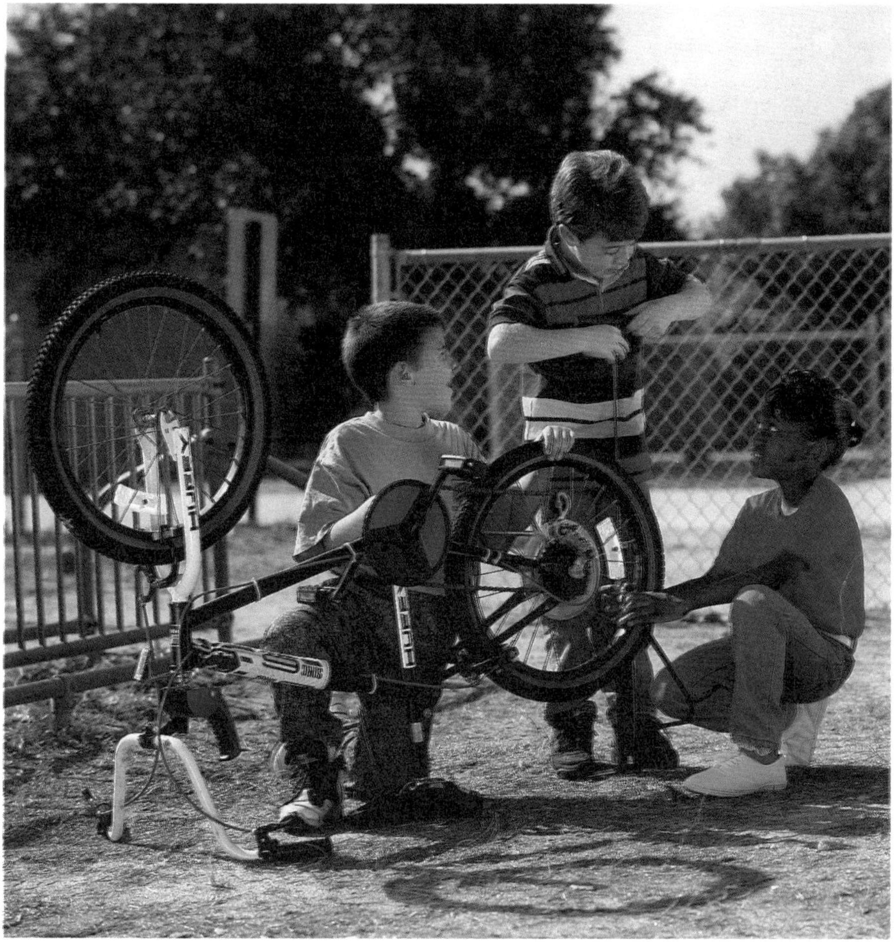

What do you do together?

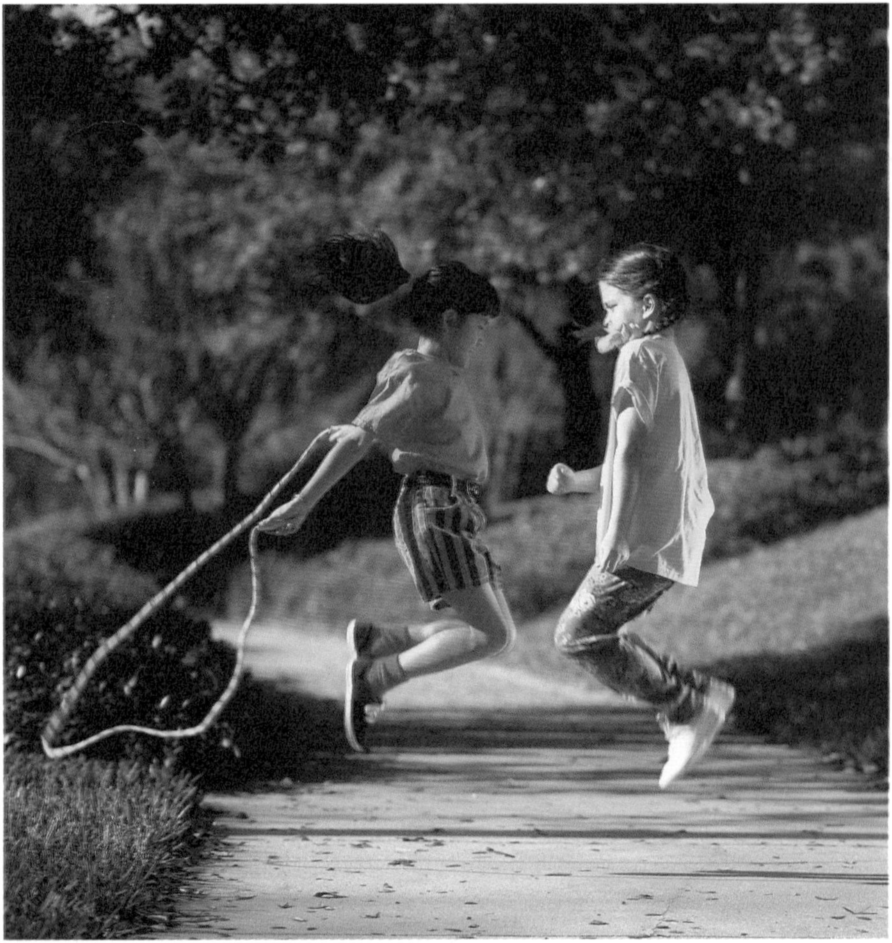